# A Streetcar Named Desire

by
Tennessee Williams

## Teacher Guide

Written by
Pat Watson

---

**Note**

The Signet, a division of Penguin Putnam, Inc., paperback edition of the drama, © The University of the South (1947, 1975), was used to prepare this guide. Page references may differ in other editions.
ISBN 0-451-16778-3

**Please note:** This drama deals with sensitive, mature issues. Parts may contain profanity, sexual references, and/or descriptions of violence. Please assess the appropriateness of this play for the age level and maturity of your students prior to reading and discussing it with them.

---

**ISBN-10:** 1-58130-950-3
**ISBN-13:** 978-1-58130-950-8
Copyright infringement is a violation of Federal Law.

© 2006 by Novel Units, Inc., Bulverde, Texas. All rights reserved. No part of this publication may be reproduced, translated, stored in a retrieval system, or transmitted in any way or by any means (electronic, mechanical, photocopying, recording, or otherwise) without prior written permission from ECS Learning Systems, Inc.

Photocopying of student worksheets by a classroom teacher at a non-profit school who has purchased this publication for his/her own class is permissible. Reproduction of any part of this publication for an entire school or for a school system, by for-profit institutions and tutoring centers, or for commercial sale is strictly prohibited.

Novel Units is a registered trademark of ECS Learning Systems, Inc.
Printed in the United States of America.

To order, contact your local school supply store, or—
Novel Units, Inc.
P.O. Box 97
Bulverde, TX 78163-0097

Web site: www.novelunits.com

**Lori Mammen,** Editorial Director
Andrea M. Harris, Production Manager/Production Specialist
A. Taylor Henderson, Product Development Specialist
Suzanne K. Mammen, Curriculum Specialist
Heather Marnan, Product Development Specialist
Pamela Rayfield, Product Development Specialist
Jill Reed, Product Development Specialist
Adrienne Speer, Production Specialist

# Table of Contents

**Summary** ................................................................3

**About the Playwright** ...........................................3

**Characters** ............................................................4

**Background Information** ....................................4

**Initiating Activities** .............................................6

**Seven Sections** ...................................................13
    Each section contains: Summary, Vocabulary,
    Discussion Questions, and Supplementary Activities

**Post-reading Discussion Questions** ...............27

**Post-reading Extension Activities** .................30

**Assessment** .........................................................31

**Scoring Rubric** ...................................................32

**Glossary** ..............................................................33

# Skills and Strategies

**Thinking**
    Analysis, compare/contrast, brainstorming, research, critical thinking, evaluation, conflict

**Vocabulary**
    Target words, definitions, application, connotation, denotation

**Writing**
    Journal, poetry, screenplay, monologue, letter

**Listening/Speaking**
    Discussion, script performance, reports, monologue

**Comprehension**
    Cause/effect, predicting, inference, plot development, thematic development, conflict resolution

**Literary Elements**
    Metaphor, simile, allusion, personification, symbolism, foreshadowing, irony, characterization, setting, theme, genre, tone, mood, juxtaposition

**Across the Curriculum**
    Music—ballad, appropriate background selections; Art—collage, caricature, diorama

**Genre:** drama

**Setting:** New Orleans, late 1940s

**Themes:** reality vs. illusion, social status, mental illness, violence, desire, deception, male chauvinism, loneliness, guilt, love, family

**Conflict:** person vs. person (Stanley vs. Blanche), person vs. self (Blanche), person vs. society (decline of way of life)

**Tone:** realistic, ironic, cynical

**Date of First Production:** December 3, 1947

## Summary

Blanche DuBois arrives at the New Orleans apartment of her sister and brother-in-law, Stella and Stanley Kowalski, for an extended visit. Blanche has been dismissed from her teaching position in Laurel, Mississippi, because of immoral conduct. She has lost the family estate and has nowhere else to go. She exists in a world of self-deception, clinging to the illusion of her past beauty and the social status of the DuBois family. Conflict erupts between Blanche and Stanley, whose cruelty ultimately destroys her last chance at happiness. She has a mental breakdown after Stanley rapes her. Stella, torn between her love and need for Stanley and her loyalty to Blanche, will not allow herself to believe Blanche's story about the rape. Blanche is left with no one to defend her. As the play draws to a close, a doctor and nurse lead Blanche away to a mental hospital.

## About the Playwright

**Personal:** Thomas Lanier Williams was born on March 26, 1911, in Columbus, Mississippi. His father, Cornelius, was a shoe salesman who came from a prestigious Tennessee family. Edwina, his mother, was the daughter of a minister. The family moved from Mississippi to St. Louis, Missouri, in 1918. He had an older sister, Rose, and a younger brother, Walter. He changed his name to "Tennessee" after moving to New Orleans after his college graduation in 1938. Williams died February 24, 1983, at the Hotel Elysee in New York City.

**Education:** In 1929, Williams began attending the University of Missouri but dropped out two years later and took a job with a shoe company. He graduated from the University of Iowa in 1938.

**Career:** Williams began writing when he was a teenager and, at the age of 16, won $5 for an essay, "Can a Good Wife Be a Good Sport?," which was published in *Smart Set*, a leading literary magazine of that era. His story, "The Vengeance of Nitocris" was published a year later in the pulp magazine *Weird Tales*. He wrote his first play, *Cairo! Shanghai! Bombay!* in 1937. Other plays followed, and in 1944 his play *The Glass Menagerie* won the New York Drama Critics' Circle Award as the best play of the season and established his reputation as a playwright. He followed this success with *A Streetcar Named Desire* in 1947. Other well-known works include *Summer and Smoke* (1948), *The Rose Tattoo* (1950), *Camino Real* (1955), *Cat on a Hot Tin Roof* (1955), *Orpheus Descending* (1957), *Suddenly Last Summer* (1958), *Sweet Bird of Youth* (1959), and *The Night of the Iguana* (1961). In addition to 30 full-length plays, Williams produced two volumes of poetry;

numerous essays, short stories, and film scripts; a novel; and a personal memoir. Several of his plays have been made into films.

**Awards:** He received two Pulitzer Prizes: *A Streetcar Named Desire* (1948), *Cat on a Hot Tin Roof* (1955). Other awards include: four New York Drama Critics' Awards, three Donaldson Awards, a Tony Award, a Medal of Honor from the National Arts Club, a Brandeis University Creative Arts Award, an $11,000 Commonwealth Award, and an honorary doctorate from Harvard University. President Jimmy Carter honored him at the Kennedy Center in 1979, and he was named a Distinguished Writer in Residence at the University of British Columbia, Vancouver, in 1981. For more information, see http://www.etsu.edu/haleyd/twbio.html (active at time of publication).

## Characters

**Blanche DuBois:** the protagonist; a fragile, destitute Southern belle who clings to an aristocratic past and lives in her own fantasy world; sexually promiscuous but wants to appear chaste; about 30 years old

**Stella Kowalski:** Blanche's younger sister; Stanley's gentle, compliant wife; has married beneath her social status; sexually enthralled with her husband

**Stanley Kowalski:** Blanche's antagonist; crude, brutal, vindictive male chauvinist; displays his sexuality; schemes to destroy Blanche

**Harold "Mitch" Mitchell:** Stanley's poker buddy and co-worker but more sensitive than Stanley; pursues Blanche but abandons her when he learns about her sordid past

**Steve and Eunice Hubbell:** friends and landlords of Stanley and Stella, who live upstairs in the same building; quarrel repeatedly but always reconcile

**Pablo Gonzales:** Stanley's poker buddy

**Young Man:** teenage newsboy; comes to collect money for the newspaper; represents Blanche's obsession with young boys

**Doctor:** comes to take Blanche to mental hospital; his kindness causes her to view him as a gallant gentleman who has come to rescue her

**Matron (Nurse):** stern; unsympathetic in her methods with Blanche

**Negro Woman:** appears in Scenes One and Ten; represents cultural diversity of New Orleans

**Mexican Woman:** sells flowers for the dead; frightens Blanche

**Allan Grey:** Blanche's young husband; poetic, sensitive; committed suicide when Blanche ridiculed him after learning of his homosexuality; died long before events in the play, but his death continues to haunt Blanche

**Shep Huntleigh:** a former suitor of Blanche, now married, whom Blanche believes will send her money to escape from Stanley; never appears onstage

## Background Information

**About the Play:** Williams identified his major plays as fitting the format of a "memory play," a three-part structure in which (1) a character experiences something profound; (2) this experience causes an "arrest of time," i.e., a situation where time loops upon itself; and (3) the character relives the experience until it makes sense to him or her. See http://www.etsu.edu/haleyd/twbio.html (active at time of publication).

**Application:** In this drama, (1) a teenage Blanche experiences deep love for her young husband and great guilt over his suicide. (2) She searches for the same love in numerous sexual encounters, culminating in her attraction to teenage boys. (3) She relives the experience each time she is faced with reality but eventually slips into insanity.

**Staging:** Williams employs realistic dialogue to reveal the depths of human nature and expressionistic staging to enhance the undercurrents of tension and illusion.

**Symbolism:** The symbolic nature of each of the following is vitally important to an understanding of the play, and these terms reappear throughout the play. These, as well as other examples of symbolism, will be noted in the applicable sections of the Discussion Questions.

1. Blanche DuBois: both names are of French origin. Blanche means *white*; DuBois means *of the wood*. Blanche is actually a contrast to the denotation of the two names. White suggests purity, and Blanche tries to portray the illusion of purity and innocence. Yet, as the play unfolds, details of her promiscuous past prove her to be the opposite. Although "of the wood" implies something firm and solid, Blanche is actually frail and easily "bent."

2. Stella: Latin term meaning *star*. To Blanche, Stella represents light in the darkness of her crumbling world. Blanche also calls Stella "Precious lamb" (see p. 19), inferring a contrast between Stella's sincerity and Blanche's deception.

3. Belle Reve: the family estate; French origin; Belle means *beautiful* and Reve means *dream*. The plantation is real and was once beautiful; however, it has deteriorated and illusions of its former grandeur are now only a dream. Blanche's loss of the estate through defaulting on a mortgage represents the loss of her own youthful dreams.

4. The streetcars Desire and Cemeteries, the area of New Orleans called Elysian Fields: terms that describe Blanche's "journey," literally and figuratively. The actual streetcar, Desire, takes her on the first stage of her journey to Stella's home. Figuratively, her desire for love and sexual fulfillment after her young husband's death takes her into a life of promiscuity. She next travels on a streetcar named Cemeteries, which figuratively represents death. Literally, Blanche has experienced the deaths of many people she loved, and figuratively, her dreams of love, protection, and wealth have died. She has now arrived at Elysian Fields, the literal street where Stella and Stanley live. Figuratively, the term is a mythological reference to Elysium, the place to which the souls of heroes were sent after death before they returned to Earth. Homer (*The Iliad*, bk. IV, l. 563) refers to the "Elysian plain at the ends of the earth." Blanche's life in the flat on Elysian Fields, where she hopes to find "new life," is the third step of her journey. It is, however, the beginning of her repetitious search for "redemption." Desire (Stanley's) sends her to a mental hospital, i.e., Cemeteries or Death.

5. Light/Darkness: Blanche's attempts to avoid light symbolize her aversion to being exposed, both literally, i.e., her age, and figuratively, i.e., her past. Light denotes the reality of her life; darkness denotes her fantasy.

6. Baths: Blanche's attempts to wash away her sordid past

7. The Blue Piano: appears in introductory stage directions and just before the last line in the play; expresses the spirit of life on Elysian Fields street; the word "blue" denotes sadness and loneliness. Throughout the play, the sound of the piano materializes when Blanche's emotions are most fragile.

8. "Varsouviana": a polka that plays when Blanche faces disastrous circumstances. This is the music to which Blanche and her young husband were dancing just before he committed suicide.

## Initiating Activities

1. Brainstorming: Place the play's title on an overhead transparency. Brainstorm with students as to possible connotations and denotations of the title.

2. Previewing: Preview the play. Note the picture on the front cover, read aloud the blurb on the back cover, and discuss the photographs that are included. Brainstorm with students as to how they think the plot will develop.

3. Film: Play the opening scene (pp. 13–31) of the 1951 movie adaptation of *A Streetcar Named Desire*: 122 minutes; B&W; Rated PG; directed by Elia Kazan; starring Vivien Leigh as Blanche, Marlon Brando as Stanley, and Kim Hunter as Stella; available on DVD. Viewing the entire DVD would be an effective way to conclude the study of the play.

4. Quotations: Place the following quote on an overhead transparency and brainstorm with students as to its significance. "It is the nature of desire not to be satisfied, and most men live only for the gratification of it" (Aristotle, *Nicomachean Ethics*, bk. II, ch. 7).

# Characterization

**Directions:** Write the name of a character from the book in the center rectangle. In each oval, write an adjective that describes the character's personality. Then fill in each dotted rectangle with a detail about the character that illustrates that part of the character's personality.

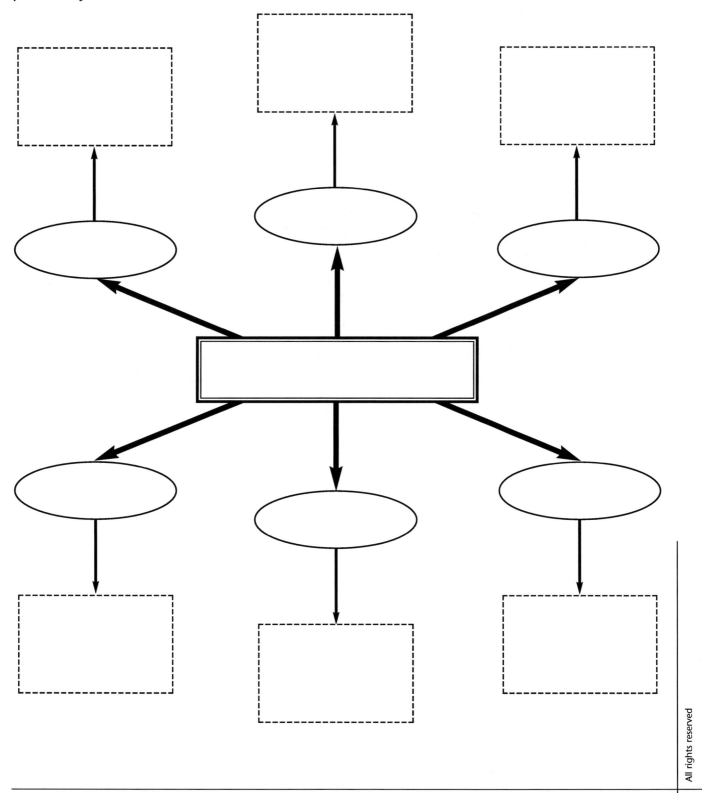

# Conflict

The **conflict** of a story is the struggle between two people or two forces. There are three main types of conflict: person vs. person, person vs. nature or society, and person vs. self.

| Character: | |
|---|---|
| **Conflict** | **Resolution** |
| | |
| | |

| Character: | |
|---|---|
| **Conflict** | **Resolution** |
| | |
| | |

| Character: | |
|---|---|
| **Conflict** | **Resolution** |
| | |
| | |

# Cause/Effect Map

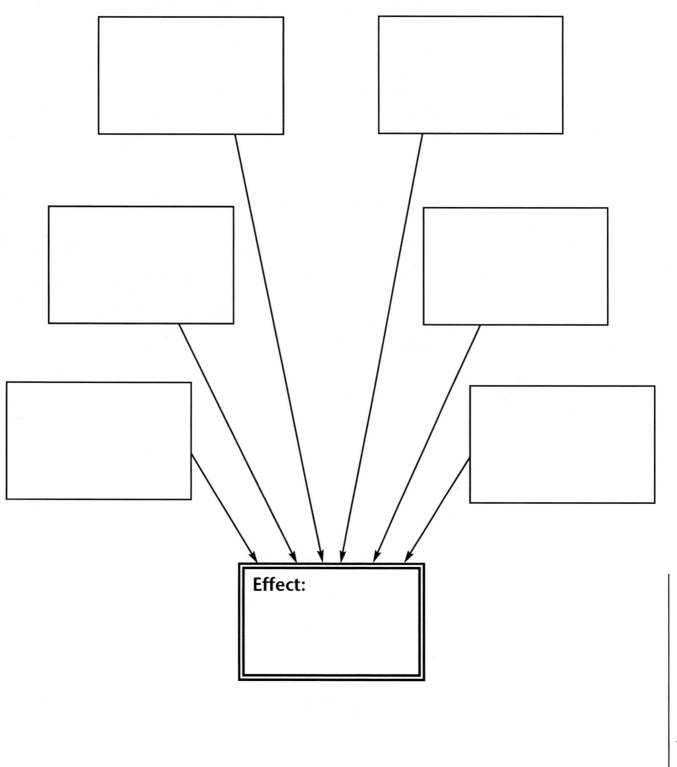

# Foreshadowing Chart

**Foreshadowing** is the literary technique of giving clues to coming events in a story.

**Directions:** What examples of foreshadowing do you recall from the story? If necessary, skim through the chapters to find examples of foreshadowing. List at least four examples below. Explain what clues are given, then list the coming event that is suggested.

| Foreshadowing | Page # | Clues | Coming Event |
|---|---|---|---|
|  |  |  |  |
|  |  |  |  |
|  |  |  |  |
|  |  |  |  |
|  |  |  |  |
|  |  |  |  |
|  |  |  |  |
|  |  |  |  |

# Story Map

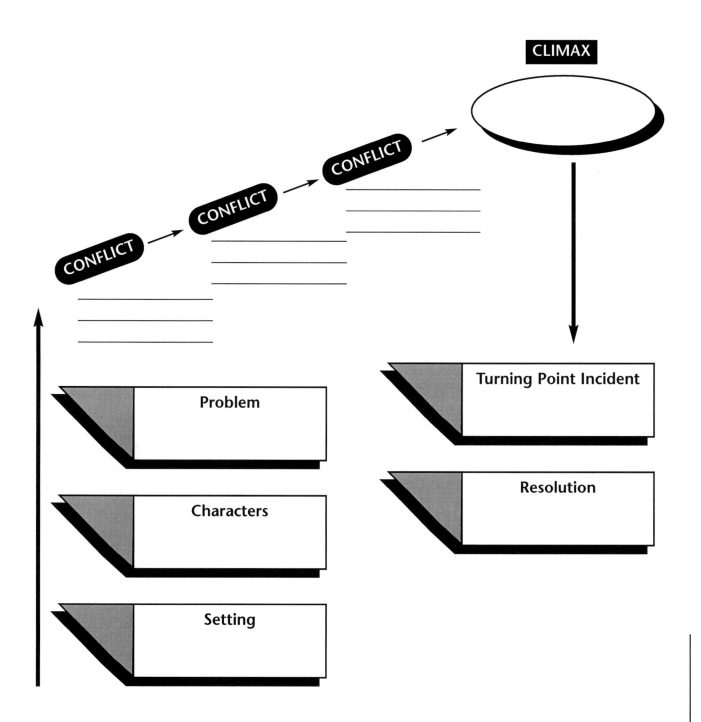

# Vocabulary Wheel

**Directions:** Write each vocabulary word on a piece of paper (one word per piece). Make a spinner using the circle below. Now play the following game with a classmate. (It is a good idea to have a dictionary and thesaurus handy.) Place the papers in a small container. The first player draws a word from the container. The player then spins the spinner and follows the direction where the pointer lands. For example, if the player draws the word "raffish" and lands on "define," the player must define the word raffish. If the player's partner accepts the answer as correct, the first player scores one point and play passes to the second player. If the player's partner challenges the answer, the first player uses a dictionary or thesaurus to prove the answer is correct. If the player can prove the answer is correct, the player earns two points. If the player cannot prove the answer is correct, the opposing player earns two points. Play continues until all the words have been used. The player with the most points wins.

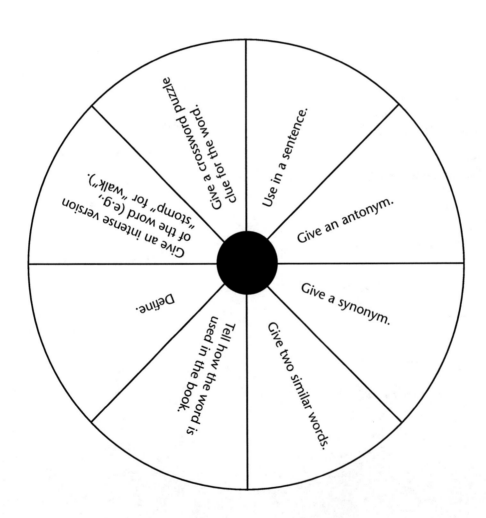

**Suggested Teaching Strategy:** Plays are written to be acted onstage, not read silently. Students will gain a deeper appreciation for *A Streetcar Named Desire* if they read it aloud. By assigning sections a day in advance, students have a chance to go over their lines and will feel more comfortable reading the play aloud in class. Because the setting is vital to the students' understanding of the drama, have a student read aloud the directions for each scene.

## Scene One, pp. 13–31

Blanche DuBois arrives for an indefinite stay with her sister, Stella, and brother-in-law, Stanley Kowalski. Blanche attributes her visit to a nervous condition that forced her to take a leave of absence from her job as a schoolteacher in Laurel, Mississippi. She reveals that she has lost the family estate, Belle Reve.

| Vocabulary |
| --- |
| raffish (13) |
| attenuates (13) |
| cosmopolitan (13) |
| incongruous (15) |
| spasmodic (18) |
| hypocritical (19) |
| dubiously (22) |
| highbrow (23) |
| heterogeneous (23) |
| implicit (29) |

### Discussion Questions

1. Discuss the setting, noting the name of the street and the significance of the two women who are sitting on the steps of the building. Observe the stage directions about the "Blue Piano" and examine the mood the setting evokes (p. 13). (*The Kowalskis live in a tiny flat in New Orleans, a city of economic and cultural diversity. This section of the city is poor but charming, and people of different races and backgrounds live here harmoniously, e.g., the friendship between the two women, one white and one black. Literally, Elysian Fields is the name of the street where Stella and Stanley live. Figuratively, the term is a mythological reference to Elysium, the section of the underworld where souls must reside before returning to Earth. New Orleans is Blanche's "Elysium," where she must live until she can find a new life. The Blue Piano appears in introductory stage directions and just before the last line in the play; the word "blue" denotes sadness and loneliness. Throughout the play, the sound of the piano materializes to express a change in the mood of the play, especially when Blanche's emotions are most fragile. p. 13*)

2. Discuss the meaning of "male chauvinist." Analyze whether or not Stanley Kowalski fits this definition. Note the metaphor describing him as a "richly feathered male bird among hens" (p. 29). (*A male chauvinist has excessive enthusiasm for his sex, race, or group. Stanley makes the living and expects Stella to serve him, gratify his desires, and never question his actions. Stanley's coarse speech and blunt behavior become evident in Scene One, where he is described as displaying "animal joy…implicit in all his movements and attitudes" [p. 29]. As the "richly feathered male bird…" his pride in his sexual prowess forms the basis of his relationships. He vigorously interacts with men, loves liquor and food, and enjoys his possessions. pp. 13–14, 23–25, 29*)

3. Examine the information about Stella and analyze her relationship with Stanley. (*In contrast to Stanley, Stella is gentle and cultured, revealing her refined ancestry. Her first onstage interaction with him sets the tone of their relationship. Stanley tosses a package of bloody meat to Stella, symbolic of a "cave man" returning from the "hunt." She protests but laughs breathlessly after catching it. She adores Stanley, is proud of his accomplishments, and accepts him as he is. Her strong sexual attraction to him supersedes his crudeness and brutality. pp. 13–14, throughout play*)

4. Discuss the information about Blanche, including her physical appearance and the reason she gives for her visit. Note the inference about her drinking. (*She is "delicately beautiful" and seems out of place in the neighborhood. When she arrives, she is dressed all in white, symbolizing the French meaning of her name [white] and the purity she attempts to portray. Her

*uncertain manner and white clothes suggest a moth [p. 15], i.e., an insect that changes in form as it develops. Blanche's journey from Belle Reve [her cocoon] to Elysian Fields is symbolic of her metamorphosis, i.e. from a protected Southern belle to a "moth" who has "flown away" and become a creature who seeks darkness to cover her age, alcoholism, and sexual promiscuity. pp. 15–19)*

5. Analyze Blanche's reaction to the setting and contrast the area with the family estate, Belle Reve. Note her reference to the "ghoul-haunted woodland of Weir" (p. 20). (*She is appalled at Stella's decline of social status, as exemplified by her apartment in a poor section of the city. Belle Reve is a plantation in Laurel, Mississippi, typifying Blanche and Stella's upbringing as members of an elite society. The "ghoul-haunted woodland of Weir" is a line from Edgar Allan Poe's poem, "Ulalume," in which the narrator roams with his Soul through an imaginary world where he finds the tomb of his lover, Ulalume. Blanche's comparison implies that she views Stella's flat as a tomb and the neighborhood as the surrounding forest. pp. 15–23*)

6. Analyze the symbolism of Blanche's travels on the two streetcars, Desire and Cemeteries, and her arrival at Elysian Fields (p. 15). (*See "Symbolism" in the Background Information on page 5 of this guide for a more complete explanation. The terms describe Blanche's "journey," literally and figuratively. The two streetcars, Desire and Cemeteries [implying death] bring her to New Orleans. She has now arrived at Elysian Fields, the literal street where Stella and Stanley live. Figuratively, Blanche hopes to find "new life" in this third step of her journey. As the plot unfolds, however, Elysian Fields becomes just another stop in her search for redemption. Ultimately, Desire [Stanley's] sends her to a mental hospital, i.e., Cemeteries or Death.*)

7. Analyze the interaction between Blanche and Stella. Note what their dialogue suggests about their relationship. (*They initially seem delighted to see each other. Blanche calls Stella by the actual meaning of her name, "Star," suggesting that she views Stella as the bright spot in her dreary world. Blanche is the more talkative of the two, indicating her role as the older sister and the spokesperson throughout their lives. Stella tries to make Blanche feel welcome but tells her that Stanley and his friends are different and cautions her not to compare Stanley with men from Laurel. She has not told Stanley about Blanche's visit. Blanche criticizes Stella's posture and her appearance, questions her about the tiny flat, and reproaches her for abandoning Belle Reve. Her attitude reflects envy of Stella's happiness and bitterness over being the one who stayed and tried to save the plantation. Blanche taunts Stella about being in bed with her "Polack" while Belle Reve was failing. pp. 18–29*)

8. Examine indications that Blanche is deceptive. What hidden truths will eventually be revealed? (*She pretends to find the liquor when, in reality, she has already had a drink from that bottle, says that one drink is her limit, and tells Stanley she rarely touches liquor. Her excuse for leaving her teaching job later proves to be a lie. She says that her reason for not going to a hotel is to be near Stella, but she actually has no money. Answers will vary. pp. 18–29*)

9. Discuss what Blanche reveals about Belle Reve and Stella's reaction, noting the importance of the "blue piano" in the stage directions. (*Blanche relates her tale of the loss of Belle Reve, telling Stella that she fought, bled, and almost died for it. During this discourse, the "blue piano" grows louder, symbolizing Blanche's emotional upheaval. Blanche is distraught and fearful of Stella's reaction and subtly blames her for leaving. She vividly portrays the deaths of their father, mother, and other relatives. While Stella returned only for the funerals, Blanche lived through the trauma of death as they struggled to breathe and begged her not to let them go. Blanche tried to save the estate, but the illnesses and burials of family members depleted the income from the plantation, and Blanche's salary could not cover the expenses. Stella is shocked and begins to cry. pp. 25–27*)

10. Examine the first meeting between Blanche and Stanley and analyze the importance of the stage directions concerning the polka (p. 31). (*Blanche hides when she hears Stanley and the other men coming in, but he sees her when he comes into the bedroom. Their initial meeting is friendly but guarded. They discuss her teaching, and he discovers that her husband died when he was quite young. The polka music rises when Stanley asks about Blanche's marriage, symbolizing Blanche's association of this type of music with her husband. She becomes ill while talking about him, foreshadowing a revelation of the tragedy of his death. pp. 29–31*)

11. **Prediction:** What will Blanche reveal about her marriage?

## Supplementary Activities

1. Based on the personification of Death as the "Grim Reaper" (p. 27), write a paragraph or a poem retelling Blanche's discourse on death from the Grim Reaper's point of view.

2. Write a journal entry in which Stella reveals her emotions about Blanche's arrival.

## Scenes Two–Three, pp. 32–61

Conflict erupts between Stanley and Blanche over the loss of Belle Reve. Blanche reveals her despair over the death of her young husband years earlier. Blanche meets Mitch when he arrives for a poker game. Stella leaves after Stanley beats her but returns when he begs for her.

| Vocabulary |
|---|
| ominously (33) |
| judicial (41) |
| absconding (41) |
| antiquity (41) |
| improvident (43) |
| fornications (43) |
| kibitz (48) |
| indolently (51) |
| portieres (57) |
| diffidently (61) |

### Discussion Questions

1. Examine the significance of the opening dialogue between Stanley and Stella. (*This scene portrays Stella's attempts to mediate between Stanley and Blanche. Stella tells Stanley about the loss of Belle Reve but tries to protect Blanche from his accusations about mishandling the funds. She cautions him that Blanche is emotionally fragile and assures him that she would never swindle anyone. Stanley's anger and resentment toward Blanche and his possessiveness of Stella are evident when he demands his "rights" under the Napoleonic code. During their conversation, however, Blanche bathes, plays, and sings, oblivious to the controversy that surrounds her. pp. 32–35*)

2. Examine the importance of Blanche's trunk. (*Stanley angrily pulls open the trunk and jerks out Blanche's things. He believes she has spent the estate money on expensive clothing and jewelry and vows to have them appraised. This scene reveals the conflict that is developing between Stanley and Stella over Blanche's presence in their small apartment and foreshadows the escalation of this tension. pp. 35–36, 41*)

3. Assess the importance of the interaction between Blanche and Stanley when she emerges from her bath. Note the color of her bathrobe. What does this scene foreshadow? (*Blanche appears dressed in a red satin robe, symbolizing her passion, contrasting with the white [for purity] she wears when she first comes to the apartment. This scene foreshadows the revelation of Blanche's sexuality and the history of her promiscuous past. After discovering that Stella is outside, she openly flirts with Stanley, asking him to button her dress, having a cigarette with him, and fishing for a compliment from him. She flatters him and then sends Stella on an errand so the two can be alone. She assures him that she understands him and is ready to answer his questions. She attempts to lighten the mood by playfully and seductively spraying him with perfume. Answers will vary. pp. 37–41*)

4. Discuss the conflict between Stanley and Blanche over the loss of Belle Reve, noting Stanley's reference to the Napoleonic code and Blanche's rationale for the plantation's downfall. (*The Napoleonic code, based on the French Civil Code, establishes the supremacy of the husband over his wife and children. Stanley refers to his rights under this code but does not take into account that the code is valid only in Louisiana, and Belle Reve is in Mississippi. Blanche tells Stanley that, although she knows she fibs a good deal, she tells the truth when something is important. She assures him that she has never cheated anyone as long as she has lived. She gives him the business papers from her box but angrily demands her letters back when Stanley grabs them. Stanley finally realizes that Blanche lost Belle Reve through default on a mortgage. When he presses her for details, she recounts how, piece-by-piece, her male ancestors impoverished the plantation through their sexual escapades. As she dumps the remaining papers on the table, she comments that it is fitting that Belle Reve, via a bunch of old papers, is now in his capable hands, implying her correlation of his sexuality with that of her relatives. Sounds of the "blue piano" after Stanley tells her about the baby symbolize Blanche's mental return to a world without conflict. pp. 40–44*)

5. Analyze the symbolism of Blanche's repeated bathing and of her aversion to light. (*Her repeated baths symbolize an attempt to wash away memories of her sordid past. She bathes when she senses conflict and/or when she is tired and nervous because bathing makes her feel "like a brand new human being." Blanche's aversion to bright light symbolizes her need to escape reality, e.g., her true age, her fading beauty, and her struggle to escape memories of her past. Her request that Mitch cover the light with a paper lantern foreshadows revelations about her husband in Scene Six and her confrontation with Mitch in Scene Nine. pp. 32, 37, 48, 55*)

6. Analyze the significance of the poker game. Note the description of the men in the stage directions at the beginning of Scene Three. (*The primary colors in which the men are dressed symbolize their masculinity and their character, i.e., bold, strong, authoritative. The scene in the Kowalski kitchen suggests reality, in contrast to Blanche's world of fantasy. The scene also serves to reveal that Mitch lives with his sick mother and is apprehensive about being alone when she dies. The men's easy camaraderie with sexual connotations indicates their earthy view of sex. When Stella and Blanche arrive, Stanley resents the intrusion into the men's concentration on the game, setting the stage for the eruption of his anger and violence. Blanche's desire for sexual attention becomes obvious when she stands, half-dressed, in the light where the men can see her. pp. 45–59*)

7. Discuss the interaction between Blanche and Mitch and what this reveals about each of them. Note Blanche's deception. (*His courtesy when Stella introduces them appeals to Blanche. Stella tells her that he is not married and lives with his mother. He is uncomfortable with Stanley's taunting about his mother. Blanche slips into her red satin robe, indicating her desire to entice Mitch. He offers her a cigarette, and their ensuing conversation about the inscription on his silver case reveals that he received it from a dying girl he loved. They dance to music from the radio. After the fight between Stanley and Stella, Mitch consoles Blanche, offering her the kindness she is searching for. Deception: Blanche, who is slightly drunk, implies that she usually drinks very little. She tells him that Stella is older than she, and she has come to help her because Stella is not well. She asks him to cover the light bulb, thus hiding her age. She tells him she teaches school in Laurel, knowing she has been fired. Blanche's allusion to her students' "making their first discovery of love" foreshadows the truth about the student with whom she was sexually involved. pp. 48–49, 52–57, 60–61*)

8. Examine Stanley's violence and analyze Stella's reaction to him. Note the significance of the background sounds (pp. 59–61). (*His slapping her on the thigh when she asks him to end the poker game indicates that he feels free to strike her when he wishes. He becomes increasingly angry*

*during the poker game. When Blanche and Mitch are dancing, he tosses the radio out the window. Stella accuses him of being drunk, calls him an "animal thing," and then runs from him. He chases her and begins to beat her, prompting the other men to restrain him and put him in the shower. He fights them, and they all leave. Subdued and remorseful, he begs for Stella, whom Blanche has taken to the Hubbells' apartment upstairs. Although Eunice threatens him and slams the door, Stella slips down the stairs to him. Their reunion symbolizes her strong sexual attraction to him. Background sounds: The combination of dissonant brass and piano sounds and the brief interval of "blue piano" music enhances the tension as Stanley begs for Stella. The music fades away as Blanche is looking for Stella, indicating the resolution of the immediate conflict. pp. 48, 52, 57–60)*

9. **Prediction:** What does the future hold for Blanche? for Stanley and Stella?

## Supplementary Activities

1. Working in small groups, do one of the following: (a) prepare a poster display of newspaper or magazine articles relating to domestic violence (b) research laws in your state concerning domestic violence (c) research the psychological dependency of men or women who have been abused on the abusing spouse (d) develop a profile of an abusive spouse. Present your results to the class.

2. Write a journal entry in which Blanche explains her statement, "I think it's wonderfully fitting that Belle Reve should finally be this bunch of old papers in your (Stanley's) big, capable hands!" (p. 43).

## Scene Four, pp. 62–73

Stella rationalizes Stanley's violence. Blanche unsuccessfully begs Stella to leave him. Stanley inadvertently overhears Blanche degrading him to Stella.

| Vocabulary |
| --- |
| bromo (69) |
| anthropological (72) |
| swilling (72) |

### Discussion Questions

1. Contrast Blanche's and Stella's reactions to Stanley's violence and analyze the significance of Stella's revelation about Stanley on their wedding night. Notice the stage directions concerning both women and contrasting their appearance. (*Blanche, concerned for Stella's safety, has spent a sleepless night and nervously approaches the apartment. Stella's sexual reconciliation with Stanley leaves her serene and contented. She cannot understand Blanche's hysterical reaction to events of the previous evening. She tries to reassure Blanche that the fight wasn't as serious as it appeared to be, that Stanley didn't know what he was doing, that he was very ashamed of himself afterward, and that he gave her ten dollars as a sign of his repentance. Her revelations about Stanley smashing all the light bulbs on their wedding night makes it obvious that violence is a part of his persona, which Stella accepts. At times, she finds it exciting. Whereas Blanche sees him as a madman, Stella sees him as the husband she loves and desires. Note: Stanley's violence followed by repentance and Stella's reaction is typical of many abusive relationships. pp. 62–64*)

2. Examine Stella's response to Blanche's concerns about her marriage. (*Blanche, determined to "save" Stella from her abusive marriage, tells her she will find a way to get her out. Stella's response is a key to the marriage, i.e., she doesn't want to get out. She accepts Stanley as he is and makes excuses for his behavior. Blanche attributes Stella's indifference to some new philosophy she's cultivated and is undeterred in her plan to take her away. Blanche's rambling reveals her own*

selfish concerns, i.e., she feels she can no longer stay in the small apartment with just the curtains between her and Stanley. Stella's and Blanche's diverse reactions to the small apartment are symbolic of the cultural differences that now exist between them. Blanche clings to dreams of money and the splendor of Belle Reve; Stella is unconcerned about the size of the apartment or Stanley's financial control as long as she can be with him. Stella laughs at Blanche's description of their situation as "desperate." pp. 64–71)

3. Discuss the information about Shep Huntleigh and how he fits into Blanche's plans. (*Shep Huntleigh symbolizes escape for Blanche and, ultimately, for Stella. Blanche dated him in college and wore his fraternity pin. [A man's "pinning a girl" was a pre-engagement promise. See p. 124 for an allusion to the ATO fraternity]. Blanche, who had gone to Miami the previous Christmas looking for "someone with a million dollars" [p. 66], had run into Shep there. He is a Texas oil millionaire, and Blanche believes he will take her and Stella to a shop of some kind even though he is married. Blanche's illusions about Huntleigh are symbolic of the fantasy world in which she tries to escape reality. pp. 66–68*)

4. Analyze Blanche's statement, "It brought me here.—Where I'm not wanted and where I'm ashamed to be" (p. 70). (*Blanche believes Stella's attraction to Stanley is based on "brutal desire," a term Blanche understands perfectly. She alludes to the streetcar, Desire, which brought her to the "end of the line," i.e., Stanley and Stella's apartment, literally and figuratively. She thinks of the literal streetcar as a rattle-trap mode of transportation in New Orleans. The figurative emotional and mental "journey" that has brought her to this point began with her desire for sexual gratification to fill the loneliness after her young husband's death. She is now destitute and lonelier than ever.*)

5. Examine what Stanley inadvertently overhears Blanche telling Stella about him. Analyze his reaction. (*The sound of an approaching train masks Stanley's presence as Blanche begins her outburst about him. She calls him "common" and refers to his bestial characteristics. She points out his "animal" habits, i.e., the way he eats, moves, and talks, and suggests that he is a sub-human survivor of the Stone Age [note the reference to Stanley's bringing home the raw meat in Scene One]. She compares his friends who gather on poker night to a party of apes who growl, snatch things, and finally fight. She concludes her attack on Stanley's character by reminding Stella of cultural things such as art, poetry, and music that have evolved since the Stone Age and begging her not to "hang back with the brutes!" [p. 72]. As another train passes by, Stanley quietly leaves and then returns, acting as if he has just arrived. Rather than confront Blanche about her tirade, Stanley hides his hatred, foreshadowing his determination to destroy her. pp. 71–73*)

6. Assess the significance of Stella's reaction to Stanley's arrival. (*In spite of his filthy clothes, she fiercely embraces him with both arms, being sure that Blanche can see them. Stanley pulls her head to him and grins at Blanche through the curtains, indicating that he knows he will win the "battle." He and Stella are "one," and Blanche is the outsider who must ultimately leave. The sounds of music symbolize the passion between Stanley and Stella. pp. 72–73*)

7. **Prediction:** How will Blanche's verbal attack on Stanley change the dynamics of the plot?

## Supplementary Activities

1. Write a metaphor poem about "Desire," based on Blanche's inference about the streetcar that brought her to this point in her life, or draw a caricature that reflects the metaphor, "His poker night…this party of apes" (p. 72).

2. Write a journal entry in which Stella records her feelings about Blanche's verbal attack on Stanley.

# Scenes Five–Six, pp. 74–96

Blanche alludes to her promiscuity and bad reputation in Laurel. Her presence in the small apartment leads to increasing tension between Stanley and Stella. Mitch is falling in love with Blanche, whom he presumes to be virtuous. Blanche reveals the details of her husband's suicide.

| Vocabulary |
|---|
| vice squad (75) |
| daemonic (75) |
| astrological (76) |
| contemptuously (77) |
| gossamer (84) |
| coquettishly (84) |
| neurasthenic (85) |
| stolid (85) |
| Bohemian (88) |
| alpaca (89) |
| effeminate (95) |

**Discussion Questions**

1. Discuss the significance of Blanche's letter to Shep Huntleigh. (*Blanche is portraying her life as she wishes it could be, traveling around the country and being entertained. Distress over Stella's marriage, anxiety about remaining under the same roof as Stanley, lack of money, and loneliness are causing Blanche to slip further into a fantasy world. p. 74*)

2. Examine the relationship between Steve and Eunice and correlate with Stanley and Stella. (*Eunice angrily confronts Steve with accusations about another woman. A fierce fight ensues, and Eunice comes downstairs, threatening to call the police, but she goes to the bar and has a drink instead. Steve, with a bruise on his head, comes downstairs. After making a sexual comment about Eunice, he goes to look for her. When they return, Steve's arm is around her, and she is sobbing while he speaks lovingly to her. They go upstairs together. Steve and Eunice's marriage mimics that of Stanley and Stella: violence followed by a sexual reunion. pp. 74–78, 81–82*)

3. Examine the cause/effect of the dialogue between Blanche and Stanley. Analyze the irony of the astrological sign under which Blanche was born and the symbolism of the thunder. (*Cause: Blanche attempts to converse with Stanley. Effect: She asks him about his astrological sign. Cause: She believes his forceful actions indicate that he was born under Aries. Effect: Stella overhears and tells her that he was born five minutes after Christmas. Cause: Blanche identifies his sign as Capricorn, the Goat. Effect: Stanley asks about her sign. Cause: She tells him she was born under Virgo, the Virgin. Effect: He contemptuously asks her about a man named Shaw [implying his knowledge of her past, identifying her as the opposite of "virgin"]. Cause: He mentions the Flamingo hotel. Effect: She implies that the hotel has a bad reputation but assures him she would never be seen in such an establishment. Cause: He taunts her by suggesting that he will have Shaw check further on the rumor. Effect: She becomes faint. Irony: A virgin has never had sexual intercourse; Blanche has had numerous sexual partners. The murmur of thunder symbolizes Steve and Eunice's passion and the approaching storm Blanche is facing. pp. 76–78*)

4. Discuss the dialogue between Blanche and Stella about Blanche's past. Note the allusion to light. (*Blanche quizzes Stella about any gossip she has heard about her, but Stella denies hearing anything. For the first time since her arrival, Blanche refers to disgraceful things she has done. She attributes her behavior to her lack of self-sufficiency and her growing older and less attractive. Blanche alludes to the need to shimmer and glow, which can be achieved by putting a paper lantern over the light to hide her fading beauty. Stella's response is to pamper Blanche by bringing her a coke with whiskey in it. Blanche emotionally thanks her and promises to leave soon, indicating her deep love for Stella, her awareness of the tension her presence is creating, and her fear that Stanley will force her out. Blanche's reaction to the spilled coke reflects her increasing emotional turmoil and instability. pp. 78–81*)

5. Analyze what Blanche tells Stella about Mitch (p. 81). Note Stella's response. (*Blanche attributes her tenseness to Mitch's imminent arrival. Her explanation to Stella about how chaste*

*she has been with Mitch reveals her deep need to find someone who loves and respects her rather than someone who just desires her sexually. She sees Mitch as the one who can rescue her from her past and from Stanley's power and provide a safe place of rest for her. She knows the truth might alienate him, and she wants to deceive him, i.e., her age and past history, enough to make him want her. Stella assures her it will happen. Although she is concerned about Blanche's drinking, she leaves to join Stanley, signifying that she is torn between her loyalty to her husband and her sister's needs. pp. 81–82)*

6. Assess the significance of Blanche's encounter with the Young Man and Mitch's arrival soon after the boy leaves. Note the allusion to Rosenkavalier (p. 84). (*After the two couples leave laughing, loneliness and boredom overwhelm Blanche, as symbolized by the slow, blue music. While she is in this state of mind, the Young Man comes to collect money for the newspaper. She offers him a drink, begins to flirt with him, and finds excuses to get him to stay. She seductively touches his shoulders. Her statement, "You make my mouth water" appears to relate to his reference to a cherry soda but actually relates to her desire for him. She flatters him and kisses him before allowing him to leave. Just as he disappears, Mitch arrives with a bouquet of roses. Blanche calls him her "Rosenkavalier," i.e., The Knight of the Rose. The term comes from the opera "Der Rosenkavalier" by Richard Strauss and refers to the presentation of a silver rose to a bride on her wedding day by the Knight of the Rose on behalf of her husband-to-be. The beautiful, married woman in the opera has a lover who is several years younger than she. Circumstances cause her to think about her flippant life, and she realizes that she is destined to lose her happiness. Blanche's allusion to Rosenkavalier symbolizes her desire for the Young Man and foreshadows the loss of her last chance at happiness. pp. 82–84)*

7. Examine the relationship between Blanche and Mitch, noting the allusion to Samson. Contrast her response to Mitch with her reaction to the newsboy. (*Blanche and Mitch return from a date to the amusement park. Blanche is exhausted and feels guilty for having been such poor company. Their dialogue reveals that she plans to leave soon and alludes to a prior date when she resisted his advances. Blanche's successful façade of a chaste single girl is evident when he tells her that he has never known anyone like her. She invites him in but insists that they leave the lights off and visit only by candlelight. She speaks to him in French, pretending they are a man and lady in Paris. When she realizes he does not understand French, she asks him if he wants to go to bed with her this evening. Their interaction is playful as she flatters him about his physique and he demonstrates his strength by lifting her. She calls him Samson, alluding to the biblical character who was the strongest man of his day. He heeds her demand that he must act like a gentleman. Her body language, i.e., rolling her eyes, when she tells him she has old-fashioned ideas reveals that her words and actions are all part of her façade. Mitch has told his mother, who wants him to be settled before she dies, about Blanche. Blanche's interaction with and expectations of Mitch contrast with the alluring, seductive way she reacts to the Young Man. pp. 85–91)*

8. Discuss Blanche's summation of why she and Stanley conflict. (*Blanche rejects Mitch's suggestion that they go out sometime with Stanley and Stella and begins to quiz him about what Stanley has said about her. She tells Mitch that Stanley is rude and offensive to her. She attributes their conflict to the lack of privacy in the small apartment and suggests that Stanley makes a point of letting her see him in his underwear. In spite of the conflict, she has no money to go anywhere else even though Stanley insults her because he hates her. She speaks of Stanley as the executioner who will destroy her, foreshadowing her ruin at his hands. pp. 92–93)*

9. Analyze what Blanche reveals about her husband. Note the reference to quicksand (p. 95) and the symbolism of the "Varsouviana" and of light (p. 96). (*She tells Mitch that she understands loneliness because she lost her husband, with whom she fell in love when she was 16. She knew he was different from other men, i.e., nervous, soft, and tender, but that he did not look*

*effeminate. After their marriage, she loved him intensely but felt like a failure because she couldn't give him the help he needed [referring to his homosexuality]. She discovered the truth when she found him in bed with an older man. The three pretended nothing had happened and drove to a casino. Her disclosure to Allan of her disgust as they were dancing to the "Varsouviana" caused him to commit suicide. Symbolism: As she tells her story, the sound of a locomotive and its glaring headlights represent her guilt and fear of exposure. Falling in love with Allan was like turning a blinding light on her world. When he died, that light was turned off in her heart, and she cannot tolerate any light stronger than a candle. The "Varsouviana" polka symbolizes disaster. When she hears it in her head, it stops only when she feels safe [it fades out when Mitch proposes to her] or when she mentally hears a gunshot [representing Allan's death]. pp. 95–96)*

10. **Prediction:** Will Mitch marry Blanche?

## Supplementary Activities

1. Write a diamante poem contrasting Light and Darkness.
2. Write a paragraph explaining your interpretation of the metaphor in Blanche's statement to the Young Man, "…an hour isn't just an hour—but a little piece of eternity dropped into your hands…" (p. 83).

## Scenes Seven–Eight, pp. 97–112

Stanley tells Stella about Blanche's promiscuous lifestyle. Mitch fails to appear for Blanche's birthday party because Stanley has told him about her past. Stanley gives Blanche her birthday present: a one-way bus ticket back to Laurel. Stella goes into labor.

| Vocabulary |
|---|
| saccharine (98) |
| contrapuntally (98) |
| contemptible (99) |
| degenerate (102) |

### Discussion Questions

1. Discuss circumstances prior to Blanche's birthday party and analyze the symbolism of her taking a long bath. (*Stanley resents Blanche's "soaking in a hot tub" all afternoon while Stella waits on her. Stella defends Blanche and accuses Stanley of deliberately antagonizing her. Stanley has been gathering information about Blanche's past and now exposes her deception to Stella. Oblivious to her imminent ruin, Blanche blithely plays like a child and sings as she bathes. Her long bath symbolizes the cleansing of all her past indiscretions in preparation for her new life with Mitch. pp. 97–100*)

2. Examine what Stanley tells Stella about Blanche. (*Lie #1: Blanche's portrayal of chastity and innocence is a façade, designed to deceive Stella and trick Mitch into marrying her. In reality, her reputation as an immoral woman in Laurel is so bad that she has been banned permanently from the Flamingo, a hotel that ordinarily does not interfere in the lives of its residents. She has gone from one man to another but can no longer get dates in Laurel, and people there consider her to be crazy. Even the army camp near Laurel lists Blanche as "out of bounds" for the soldiers. Lie #2: Blanche has been fired from her teaching position in Laurel because of her sexual indiscretion with a 17-year-old student. Blanche came to stay with Stella because she had nowhere else to go. pp. 98–101*)

3. Assess the effect of Stanley's revelations about Blanche. Note the symbolism of the background music. (*Stella initially believes Stanley's informant is lying. She tries to explain that Blanche's behavior has always been unpredictable but attributes her emotional instability to the discovery of her husband's homosexuality. Stella is dismayed to learn that Stanley has told Mitch*

*the truth about Blanche and wonders what will happen to her now. Stanley, in an uncharacteristic move, gently takes Stella by the shoulders, but Stella withdraws from him. He reveals that he has purchased a one-way bus ticket for Blanche to leave. Blanche, who emerges from her bath refreshed and excited, realizes something is wrong when Stella responds to her in a sad, doubtful voice. Blanche fearfully demands to know what has happened. The blue piano in the background "goes into a hectic breakdown," symbolizing Blanche's imminent mental and emotional breakdown. pp. 101–105)*

4. Analyze the juxtaposition of "Paper Moon" with Stanley's revelations about Blanche's past. Complete lyrics for "Paper Moon" by Ella Fitzgerald are available at www.lyricsfreak.com/e/ell-fitzgerald/45646.html (active at time of publication). (*Blanche sings about the phony "Paper Moon," with each verse ending in "But it wouldn't be make-believe If you believed in me." Symbolically, she has now found someone [Mitch] who believes in her and can replace her fantasy world with reality. Even as she sings in the background, however, the playwright juxtaposes Stanley's cruel revelation of her shameful past to Stella. He has also exposed Blanche to Mitch, thus destroying her last chance at happiness. pp. 98–101)*

5. Discuss the aftermath of Blanche's birthday party. Note the stage directions regarding Stanley, Stella, and Blanche at the beginning of Scene Eight. (*Stanley feels justified in his exposure of Blanche; Stella is embarrassed over what she has learned and is sad for Blanche; Blanche is strained but puts on a "tight, artificial smile." The empty place at the table indicates that Mitch has not come. Blanche tries to lighten the tension by asking Stanley to tell a joke, and then tells one of her own when he refuses. Conflict erupts between Stella and Stanley over his eating habits, and he reacts violently when Stella tells him what to do. He hurls his plate to the floor, grabs her arm, and commands her never to speak that way to him because he is the king in their house. After he stalks out, Blanche begs Stella to tell her what he has told her and why Mitch has not come. She unsuccessfully attempts to call Mitch. Stanley and Blanche clash over her extended use of the bathroom and her referring to him as a "Polack." He gives her a one-way bus ticket back to Laurel as a birthday present. pp. 106–110)*

6. Analyze the resolution of Stanley and Stella's current conflict, noting the real reason for Stanley's resentment of Blanche. (*Stella joins him outside and stares reproachfully at him, but he turns away from her. After she begins to cry, he takes her in his arms and assures her that it will be all right after Blanche leaves and Stella has the baby. He comes back into the kitchen as Stella prepares to light the candles on Blanche's birthday cake. This scene reveals Stanley's deep resentment over Blanche's presence in the small apartment. Because only the curtains separate her from him and Stella at night, she hinders their love life. Stella is torn between her love for Stanley and her sense of responsibility for Blanche. pp. 108–109)*

7. Discuss Blanche's and Stella's reactions to the bus ticket and analyze Stanley's rationale for giving it to Blanche. Note the symbolism of the "Varsouviana" in the stage directions. (*Blanche initially protests that she didn't expect a gift. When she realizes his "gift" is a one-way bus ticket back to Laurel, she unsuccessfully tries to laugh and smile. She then runs into the bathroom and begins to throw up. Stella reproaches Stanley for his cruelty and blames the abuse of men like him for Blanche's decline from a tender, trusting young girl to her present status. Stella demands to know why he did this. Stanley reminds her that she, too, once thought he was common, but she changed her opinion when they fell in love. He implies that he believes Blanche has destroyed their happiness; therefore, he wants to destroy her. The "Varsouviana," which had faded out when Mitch proposed to Blanche at the end of Scene Six, begins softly when Stanley gives Blanche the bus ticket, symbolizing the return of her hopelessness, fear, and guilt. pp. 110–112)*

8. **Prediction:** What will happen to Blanche now?

## Supplementary Activities

1. Working in a small group, re-enact the birthday party and its aftermath.
2. Write a short monologue in which Blanche reacts to the one-way bus ticket back to Laurel.

## Scenes Nine–Ten, pp. 113–130

Mitch confronts Blanche about her deception. Blanche admits her sexual indiscretions, and Mitch declares her not clean enough to marry. Stanley, who is drunk, returns from the hospital because Stella's baby will not be born until morning. His cruel confrontation with Blanche about her lies sends her over the edge mentally. He rapes her.

### Vocabulary

uncavalier (113)
recriminations (119)
spectral (122)
transitory (126)
*sinously (128)
*spelling in text

### Discussion Questions

1. Evaluate the importance of the stage directions at the beginning of Scene Nine. (*Blanche's body language, i.e., tense and hunched over, indicates her distraught state of mind. She wears her red robe, symbolizing the thwarted passionate desire that has consumed her since Allan's death. She is drinking to escape the mental sounds of the "Varsouviana," which symbolizes the same sense of disaster she felt when Allan committed suicide. This sets the stage for Mitch's arrival and their ensuing confrontation. p. 113*)

2. Analyze why Blanche tells Mitch, "You've stopped that polka tune that I had caught in my head" (p. 113), and examine the implications of his coming to the apartment. (*Blanche ceases to hear the tune in her head because Mitch's appearance symbolizes the renewal of her hope for a better life. She attempts to recapture the façade by hiding her liquor bottle and repairing her makeup. She becomes fearful when he fails to respond to her offer of a kiss and reproves him for his appearance and aloofness, but quickly forgives him. She does everything she can to please him but continues to try to deceive him by implying that she does not know where to find the liquor. The polka tune starts again when he fails to respond to her overtures but dies out again when she mentally hears the gunshot that ended Allan's life. Mitch has obviously come to the apartment to expose Blanche's deception, e.g., his reference to her lapping up Stanley's liquor all summer and his determination to see her in the light. pp. 113–121*)

3. Analyze the symbolism of dark and light in this scene, correlating Blanche's statement, "I don't want realism. I want magic!" (p. 117). (*Blanche prefers the dark, which hides her age and her fading beauty. The darkness of lies enables her to escape the memories and hide from her past. Light, literally and figuratively, exposes Blanche. Only in the dark can she find the magic for which she is searching; the light symbolizes the realism that obliterates the magic. She has hidden her true age by refusing to go out with Mitch in the afternoon, by insisting they go to dimly lighted places at night, and by covering the light bulb with a paper lantern. Mitch reveals her age by tearing off the lantern, thus exposing her face to the bare light. The "light of truth" exposes Blanche's past and destroys the persona with which Mitch fell in love. She admits that she lies, telling what should be the truth in order to give people "magic." In the light, however, Blanche's "house of lies" crumbles. pp. 116–117*)

4. Discuss what Blanche tells Mitch about her past, noting the symbolism of the Tarantula Arms and the reference to the "tail of the kite." (*After Mitch tells her that two other men have corroborated Stanley's tales about her, she relates her version of the story. She refers to the Tarantula*

*[spider] Arms [hotel] and herself as the big spider who lured her victims to the hotel. She acknowledges having been intimate with many strangers but attributes this to her need to fill the emptiness left in her heart by Allan's death. Her search culminated in the seduction of a boy close to Allan's age when they married. Realizing that her youth was gone and she was "unfit," she came to Stella because she had nowhere else to go. She feels that she and Mitch were destined for each other because of their mutual need, that he represents her safe refuge, and that together they can rise above their hurt [like a kite]. The kite cannot soar now, however, because her three adversaries have tied an old tin can [her past] to its tail. pp. 117–119)*

5. Examine the resolution of Mitch's confrontation with Blanche. Analyze the symbolism of the blind Mexican woman. (*Mitch cannot forgive Blanche for lying to him. Blanche believes her own deception, i.e., she did not lie in her heart. When the Mexican woman arrives selling "flores para los muertos," i.e., flowers for the dead, memories from Blanche's past sweep over her, symbolizing death. Mentally, she sees again the deaths of her relatives at Belle Reve and hears the recriminations from those who were dying. Blanche replaced "death" with "desire," and sexual intimacy with the young soldiers from a nearby camp became her escape from the death that surrounded her at Belle Reve. Mitch's attempt to get her to satisfy his sexual desire, followed by his refusal to marry her because she is not clean enough to be in a house with his mother, symbolizes the death of her fantasy and sends her "over the edge" mentally. pp. 119–121*)

6. Analyze Blanche's appearance, mental state, and monologue at the beginning of Scene Ten. (*Her drunkenness and packing have caused her to become hysterically exhilarated. The way she is now dressed, as if she is a princess ready for a formal ball, symbolizes her retreat into her own world of delusion. She speaks to herself as if she is at the ball, wondering what to do next for excitement. Her reaction when she looks at herself in the mirror [slamming it down violently and moaning] indicates her vacillation between fantasy and reality. p. 122*)

7. Examine the dialogue between Stanley and Blanche. (*They have both been drinking. His reply to Blanche's question about Stella and the baby, i.e., the baby won't come until morning, makes her anxious when she realizes they will be alone for the night. She lies about her appearance, telling him that Shep Huntleigh has invited her to go on a Caribbean cruise and that she has been going through her trunk to find suitable clothing. Stanley removes his shirt and suggests they have a drink together, bury the hatchet, and make it a loving cup. He gets his silk pajamas that he wore on his wedding night, telling Blanche that he will wave the top like a flag when the telephone rings and he hears that he has a son. These actions, plus his comment that it is a "red letter night" for both of them, foreshadow the rape that ends this scene. pp. 122–125*)

8. Analyze Blanche's improvisation about Shep Huntleigh and her lies about Mitch. (*She tells Stanley that Shep is a gentleman who respects her and wants only her companionship. She portrays herself as a woman whom a man like Shep would desire, i.e., cultivated and intelligent, with beauty of the mind, richness of the spirit, and tenderness of the heart. The allusion to casting her pearls before swine [Bible, Matthew 7:6] indicates her regret for losing her virtue to unworthy men. She classifies Stanley and Mitch as swine and proceeds to lie to Stanley about Mitch's reasons for coming to see her. She tells him that Mitch came to repeat the vicious stories about her, and that she sent him away but he returned with a box of roses to beg her forgiveness. She continues her lie with an untruth about Mitch's deliberate cruelty and her refusal to forgive him. Stanley leaves her defenseless and frightened by cruelly confronting her with the lies about Shep and Mitch and taunting her about her ridiculous appearance. pp. 124–128*)

9. Analyze the implications of the final confrontation between Stanley and Blanche, noting the symbolism of the background images and sounds. (*Immediately after Stanley confronts Blanche about her lies, grotesque, menacing reflections appear on the wall around Blanche.*

*Inhuman voices like cries in a jungle are added to the lurid reflections while she is on the phone begging the operator to put her in touch with Shep Huntleigh. The back walls of the rooms have become transparent, and a prostitute is seen struggling with a drunkard, followed by the Negro Woman going through the prostitute's bag. As Stanley emerges from the bathroom in his silk pajamas, the blue piano becomes louder and turns into the roar of an approaching train. The sounds and images symbolize Blanche's descent into insanity and her inevitable final conflict with Stanley, i.e., the rape. Blanche attempts to leave and then to defend herself with a broken whiskey bottle, but she cannot escape the "destiny" that has been hers from the day she first met Stanley, as indicated by his final line in this scene. pp. 128–130)*

## Supplementary Activities

1. Write a paragraph in which you explain your interpretation of Stanley's last line in Scene Ten, "We've had this date with each other from the beginning!" (p. 130).

2. Write a journal entry that reflects Blanche's emotions after Mitch leaves.

## Scene Eleven, pp. 131–142

Blanche believes she is going away for a rest in the country with Shep Huntleigh. The doctor and nurse arrive to take her to the mental hospital. Stella convinces herself that Blanche's story about the rape is untrue.

| Vocabulary |
| --- |
| prodigiously (131) |
| quinine (136) |
| aura (136) |
| affectedly (137) |
| colloquy (137) |
| sotto voce (139) |
| voluptuously (142) |

### Discussion Questions

1. Discuss the importance of the setting for this scene. Note the significance of the poker game and what the conversation between Stella and Eunice reveals. (*A few weeks have passed since Stanley raped Blanche. Blanche is bathing while Stella, who has been crying, packs her things. The four men involved in the poker game present the same scenario as the night Stanley beat Stella at the beginning of the play. Stanley is unconcerned and going on with his life as if nothing happened between him and Blanche. Mitch's frustration indicates his resentment toward Stanley for destroying his chance at happiness with Blanche. The dialogue between Stella and Eunice reveals that Eunice has been keeping Stella's baby so Stella could pack Blanche's things. Stella has told Blanche she is going for a rest in the country, and Blanche thinks she will be with Shep Huntleigh. Blanche's bathing and choice of clothing indicate that she wants to look her best for this journey. Stella's words to Eunice, "I couldn't believe her story and go on living with Stanley" [p. 133] reveal that, although she weeps over Blanche's plight, she cannot continue to live with Stanley if she believes her story about the rape. pp. 131–133*)

2. Discuss the significance of Blanche's first appearance onstage in this scene. (*She is dressed in her red satin robe and reflects a tragic radiance. The accompanying sounds of the "Varsouviana" symbolize that Blanche has lost her struggle with insanity and once again is consumed with memories of betrayal and guilt. Stanley's voice shocks her out of her trance-like state and triggers hysteria as she becomes aware that something sinister is going on around her. She demands an explanation, but Stella soothes her into compliance. She wants to get dressed and be ready when Shep arrives. pp. 133–135*)

3. Contrast Blanche's vision about what is going to happen with the truth. (*The cathedral chimes, which symbolize cleanliness to Blanche, supersede the "Varsouviana," which fades into the*

*background. Blanche fantasizes about her trip. She foresees herself dying and being buried at sea in a clean white sack, falling into an ocean as blue as Allan's eyes. In contrast, the approach of the Doctor and Matron denote reality, for they have come to take Blanche to the mental hospital. Blanche is hesitant and apprehensive when she hears the doorbell and realizes someone has come for her, especially when she learns that both a man and a woman have arrived. She tries to stall when she realizes the man is not Shep. Symbolically, the cathedral chimes have ceased and only the "Varsouviana" is playing in the distance. Blanche recognizes that something is wrong and rushes back into the bedroom, saying she has forgotten something. The "Varsouviana" becomes distorted and is accompanied by lurid reflections on the walls as she seizes a chair in an attempt to defend herself. The Matron and Stanley start toward her, and she begs to be left alone. Stanley strikes the final blow to her sanity by tearing the paper lantern off the light bulb. She reacts as if she is being torn the same way. She screams and tries to escape, but the Matron restrains her. The Doctor and Matron ultimately lead her away. pp. 134–142)*

4. Analyze the Doctor's calming effect on Blanche. (*He becomes more personal to her when he takes off his hat and speaks gently and reassuringly to her. Her terror subsides, and she becomes calm when he speaks her name, as symbolized by the cessation of the inhuman cries and noises in the background. Blanche trusts the Doctor because he is kind, and she has "always depended on the kindness of strangers." She leaves with him without looking back and refuses to respond to Stella, who repeatedly calls her name. pp. 141–142)*

5. Discuss the reaction of the other characters to incidents leading up to Blanche's departure. Why do you think each character reacts in this way? (*Mitch at first remains seated and stares down at the table but later starts toward the bedroom. When Stanley blocks his way, he pushes him aside and strikes at him and then collapses, sobbing. Stanley initially tries to pacify Blanche by telling her he will send her things later, but he subsequently lashes out at her and tears down the lantern. Stella begs Eunice not to let the Doctor and Matron hurt Blanche. She realizes she is responsible for what is happening to Blanche. Eunice assures Stella that this is the only thing Stella can do because Blanche has nowhere else to go. Answers will vary. pp. 138–141)*

6. Analyze the final scene between Stella and Stanley. (*Stella, sobbing intensely, takes her baby from Eunice. Stanley stands at the foot of the steps looking at her. When he uncertainly speaks her name, her sobs become more convulsive. He speaks gently and kneels beside her. The reference to his fingers finding the opening of her blouse, accompanied by the rising music of the Blue Piano, imply that she will again find comfort in his sexual embrace. p. 142)*

## Supplementary Activity

1. Working in small groups, respond to one of the following: (a) write a scene about Stella and Stanley one week after Blanche leaves (b) write a monologue explaining Mitch's reactions to Blanche's departure (c) write a psychiatric report of Blanche the week after she arrives at the mental hospital (d) create a collage depicting Blanche's emotional state in the final scene.

# Post-reading Discussion Questions

1. Using the Characterization chart on page 7 of this guide, evaluate each of the following characters: Blanche, Stanley, Stella, Mitch. (*Blanche: fragile—lack of stamina at carnival; deceptive—lies about teaching job; nymphomaniacal—lurked outside army camp for sexual liaisons; destitute—owns only what is in her trunk; lonely—drinks to fill emptiness; fearful—reaction to allusions about her past. Stanley: uncouth—appalling table manners; violent—beats Stella; volatile—easily angered during card game; controlling—will not allow Stella to contradict him; sensual—physical build and conversation convey sexuality; vindictive—determined to destroy Blanche. Stella: compliant—submits to Stanley's authority; perceptive—aware of Blanche's distress; thoughtful—waits on Blanche; easygoing—doesn't get upset easily; amorous—sexually enthralled with Stanley; contented—accepts life in small apartment. Mitch: lonely—dreads being alone when his mothers dies; gentle—treats Blanche tenderly until he finds out about her past; considerate—takes care of his mother; sensitive—dislikes Stanley's overt manner with women; truthful—cannot accept Blanche's lies about her past; reserved—not always able to relay his true feelings.*)

2. Using the Conflict chart on page 8 of this guide, examine the following conflicts: Blanche vs. society; Blanche vs. Stanley; Blanche vs. herself. Note that Blanche is the "loser" in the resolution of each conflict. (*Society: her sexual liaisons in her search for something to fill her loneliness; Resolution: Society rejects her; she loses her teaching job. Stanley: his resentment over cramped living conditions after Blanche arrives; his sexual desire for her; Resolution: He destroys her last chance for happiness [with Mitch]; he rapes her, adding the final blow to her mental instability. Herself: her struggles to erase the guilt over Allan's death and to fill the loneliness; deception; Resolution: She ultimately destroys herself; slips over the edge into insanity.*)

3. Using the Cause/Effect Map on page 9 of this guide, write "Blanche's mental collapse" in the "Effect" box and analyze the causes leading up to this effect. (*Causes: [1] Allan's suicide [2] repeated sexual promiscuity [3] resentment toward Stella for leaving Belle Reve [4] tending to numerous relatives as they died [5] losing Belle Reve [6] being raped by Stanley*)

4. Using the Foreshadowing Chart on page 10 of this guide, discuss examples of foreshadowing throughout the play. (*Stanley throws the meat at Stella: his animalistic behavior; Blanche takes a drink, then pretends to look for liquor after Stella arrives: Blanche's alcoholism; Stanley goes through Blanche's trunk: his determination to destroy her; Blanche flirts with and flatters Stanley: her desperation for a place to stay; Stanley tells Blanche that he might get ideas about her if she weren't his wife's sister: his sexual attraction for her and the eventual rape; Stanley hits Stella on the thigh: his propensity for violence; Blanche hates light: revelation of her deception; Stella returns to Stanley after he beats her: she will choose him over Blanche regardless of the circumstances; Stanley overhears Blanche denigrating him to Stella: he will find a way to destroy her; Stanley mentions hearing about the Flamingo hotel from a man named Shaw: the revelation of Blanche's past; Mitch fails to come for Blanche's birthday supper: his rejection of her; a blind Mexican woman sells flowers for the dead: Blanche's figurative death*)

5. Using the Story Map on page 11 of this guide, analyze the plot of the play. (*Setting: New Orleans; Characters [primary]: Blanche DuBois, Stanley and Stella Kowalski, "Mitch" Mitchell; Problem: Blanche's need to escape her past and find happiness; Conflict: [1] Blanche's loss of Belle Reve [2] her need of a place to stay [3] Stanley's resentment of her presence in the small apartment; Climax: Stanley rapes Blanche. Turning Point Incident: [1] Stanley overhears Blanche degrading him. [2] Stanley reveals truth about Blanche's past; Resolution: Blanche loses her hold on sanity and is sent to a mental hospital.*)

6. Analyze the symbolism of the following: Light/Dark, Thunder, the Blue Piano, the "Varsouviana" polka. (*Light/Dark: Light symbolizes the truth and reality; therefore, Blanche hates*

*the light. Darkness [or a dim light] hides her literal age and allows her to escape reality. When Mitch snatches the paper lantern from the light bulb, Blanche's true age is revealed. Figuratively, she must also face her own deception. Blanche refers to falling in love with her husband like "turning on a blinding light"; Allan's death caused the darkness to descend on her life. To Stanley, light symbolizes exposure of anything false. Thunder: symbolizes the escalating "storm" in Blanche's life. The Blue Piano "expresses the spirit of the life which goes on here," i.e., in New Orleans [p. 13]. The piano signals change in the dynamics of scenes, i.e., loud or soft. Its appearance when Blanche talks about losses in her life symbolizes her loneliness, e.g., the piano is "slow and blue" when Mitch rejects her [p. 121]. The "Varsouviana" symbolizes Blanche's past, e.g., she and Allan were dancing to the polka when she revealed her disgust for him which led to his suicide. The music reappears when Blanche faces disaster, e.g., when Stanley gives her a one-way ticket back to Laurel and as she dresses for her "trip" to the mental hospital.)*

7. Discuss whether or not the ending harmonizes with the playwright's portrayal of Blanche, Stanley, Stella, and Mitch. (*Blanche is portrayed throughout the play as fragile [mentally and physically], deceptive, and lonely. In the final scene, her mental fragility has deteriorated into insanity; she continues to believe a lie, i.e., that Shep Huntleigh is coming for her; and she faces the loneliest phase of her life without relatives or friends. Her path of self-destruction has ended. The cruel, self-centered persona Stanley has portrayed throughout is obvious in the final scene. He has achieved his goal, Blanche's ruin. He goes on with life as if nothing has happened even though he is the cause of Blanche's destruction and torments her to the end, e.g., tearing the paper lantern from the light bulb and thrusting it at her. Stella's portrayal as a compliant wife and a sister who loves but offers little help continues to the end. She refuses to acknowledge the truth about the rape, choosing her life with Stanley over any obligation to her sister. Blanche must face her future in the mental hospital alone much as she faced the deaths of everyone at Belle Reve alone. Mitch remains the same quiet, unassuming man he is when Blanche first meets him. Although he is distraught over the way she is being treated, he does little to defend her. He ineffectively attempts to get to her but collapses, sobbing, when Stanley pushes him aside. He is contrite over his part in her mental collapse but cannot bring himself to forgive her.*)

8. Analyze the development of the theme of deception throughout the play. (*Blanche hides her alcoholism and lies about why she has left her teaching position, saying that the superintendent suggested she take a leave of absence. She has no money but tells Stella she won't stay in a hotel because she wants to be near her. Blanche deceives Mitch about her age, hides her past, pretends to be chaste, and tells him that she is Stella's younger sister. Her self-deception includes her dream that Shep Huntleigh will rescue her and her rationale for "fibbing." Stanley hides the fact that he overheard Blanche's tirade about him. Stella lies when she tells Blanche that she doesn't know why Mitch has not arrived for the birthday supper. Blanche lies about going on a cruise with Shep and about Mitch's remorse for not coming to her birthday supper. Everyone lies to Blanche about where she is going and why. Stella tries to deceive herself into believing that Blanche's story of the rape is a lie.*)

9. Compare/contrast Stanley and Mitch. (*Both work hard to provide living expenses—Stanley for Stella, Mitch for his mother. They are about the same age and served in the army together. Both enjoy playing poker and drinking [Stanley more than Mitch]. Stanley has a wife who loves him; Mitch is lonely. Stanley is self-centered, demanding, authoritative, cruel, violent, callous, and insensitive. Mitch is concerned for others, compliant, dutiful, gentle, kind, and compassionate.*)

10. Compare/contrast Blanche and Stella. (*Both were raised in the refined atmosphere of Belle Reve. Blanche stayed at the plantation; Stella left. Both have a strong sexual desire; however, Blanche desires many men and Stella desires only Stanley. Blanche is talkative, lonely, and deceptive; Stella is reticent, content, and honest. Blanche longs to return to the "glory" of plantation life; Stella is content in a small apartment in New Orleans.*)

11. Analyze the symbolism of the title. (*A streetcar named Desire takes Blanche on the first part of her journey to New Orleans. This establishes "desire" as a primary theme of the play. Blanche's desire for sexual gratification causes her to lose self-respect and her reputation, i.e., to become known as morally unfit. It eventually leads to the loss of her teaching position. Blanche's allusion to the "epic fornications" of her ancestors implies that sexual desire ultimately led to the loss of Belle Reve. Stanley and Stella's marriage is built more on sexual desire than on unconditional love. Stanley's desire for Blanche culminates in rape and is the final blow to Blanche's fragile emotional and mental condition.*)

# Post-reading Extension Activities

**Writing/Speaking**
1. Write and give an oral performance of Stella presenting a monologue as she stands alone onstage the morning after Blanche is taken away.
2. Write a diamante poem contrasting "Illusion" with "Reality."
3. Write a metaphor poem of 8–12 lines about "Deception."
4. Write a letter from Blanche to Stella six months after the end of the play.

**Drama/Music**
1. Working with a small group, write and stage a different ending for the play.
2. Working with a small group, stage a dramatic portion of one scene. Use appropriate lighting and music.
3. Working with a small group, write and stage a scene in which Blanche arrives at the Kowalski home one year after the play ends.

**Art**
1. Create a collage depicting the symbolism of Light and Dark in the play.
2. Draw a caricature portraying Stanley as Blanche describes him to Stella (see p. 72).
3. Create a diorama of the stage setting.

**Research**
1. Research mental illness and identify the type of illness from which you think Blanche suffers. Share your findings with the class.

# Assessment for *A Streetcar Named Desire*

Assessment is an ongoing process. The following ten items can be completed during the novel study. Once finished, the student and teacher will check the work. Points may be added to indicate the level of understanding.

Name _____ Date _____

**Student**     **Teacher**

_____    _____    1. Write three questions you would ask Blanche (based on her past) if you were the psychiatrist who interviews her when she arrives at the mental hospital. Exchange with a partner and answer the questions.

_____    _____    2. After the class is divided into two teams, play the "Vocabulary Wheel" game on page 12 of this guide.

_____    _____    3. Draw the name of a character from a box and respond orally to each of the following questions about your character: (1) What is his or her role in the play? (2) What kind of person is he or she? (3) What about this character makes him or her liked or disliked? (4) How do you explain his or her actions? (5) What would you do differently if you were this character?

_____    _____    4. Choose a theme from the play and explain to the class how it is developed, e.g., reality vs. illusion, mental illness, violence, male chauvinism, guilt, deception, desire.

_____    _____    5. Correct all quizzes taken over the novel.

_____    _____    6. Share your Post-reading Extension Activity from page 30 of this guide with the class on the assigned day.

_____    _____    7. Write a review of the play for the school newspaper. Use at least ten of the vocabulary words.

_____    _____    8. Write a bio-poem for Blanche or Stanley.

_____    _____    9. Write a paragraph explaining the development and resolution of one type of conflict in the play.

_____    _____    10. Share any vocabulary, comprehension, or literary analysis activities you have completed during the study of this play.

# Linking Novel Units® Lessons to National and State Reading Assessments

During the past several years, an increasing number of students have faced some form of state-mandated competency testing in reading. Many states now administer state-developed assessments to measure the skills and knowledge emphasized in their particular reading curriculum. The discussion questions and post-reading questions in this Novel Units® Teacher Guide make excellent open-ended comprehension questions and may be used throughout the daily lessons as practice activities. The rubric below provides important information for evaluating responses to open-ended comprehension questions. Teachers may also use scoring rubrics provided for their own state's competency test.

*Please note:* The Novel Units® Student Packet contains optional open-ended questions in a format similar to many national and state reading assessments.

## Scoring Rubric for Open-Ended Items

| | |
|---|---|
| **3-Exemplary** | Thorough, complete ideas/information<br>Clear organization throughout<br>Logical reasoning/conclusions<br>Thorough understanding of reading task<br>Accurate, complete response |
| **2-Sufficient** | Many relevant ideas/pieces of information<br>Clear organization throughout most of response<br>Minor problems in logical reasoning/conclusions<br>General understanding of reading task<br>Generally accurate and complete response |
| **1-Partially Sufficient** | Minimally relevant ideas/information<br>Obvious gaps in organization<br>Obvious problems in logical reasoning/conclusions<br>Minimal understanding of reading task<br>Inaccuracies/incomplete response |
| **0-Insufficient** | Irrelevant ideas/information<br>No coherent organization<br>Major problems in logical reasoning/conclusions<br>Little or no understanding of reading task<br>Generally inaccurate/incomplete response |

# Glossary

**Scene One, pp. 13–31**
1. raffish (13): showy and cheap; tawdry
2. attenuates (13): eases; makes less obvious
3. cosmopolitan (13): international; worldly; free from national and local prejudices
4. incongruous (15): not appropriate; out of place
5. spasmodic (18): sudden; showing bursts of excitement
6. hypocritical (19): insincere; two-faced
7. dubiously (22): doubtfully; uncertainly
8. highbrow (23): a person who cares, or claims to care, a great deal about knowledge and culture
9. heterogeneous (23): different in kind; varied
10. implicit (29): understood; unspoken

**Scenes Two–Three, pp. 32–61**
1. ominously (33): unfavorably; threateningly
2. judicial (41): legal; having to do with a court of law
3. absconding (41): going away hurriedly and secretly
4. antiquity (41): old age; the distant past
5. improvident (43): not looking ahead; careless in preparing for the future
6. fornications (43): acts of voluntary sexual intercourse between unmarried persons; acts of adultery
7. kibitz (48): to watch a card game
8. indolently (51): listlessly; lazily
9. portieres (57): curtains hung across doorways
10. diffidently (61): lacking self-confidence; shyly

**Scene Four, pp. 62–73**
1. bromo (69): remedy for headache and indigestion; contains sodium bicarbonate
2. anthropological (72): having to do with the science that deals with man's physical characteristics, the origin and development of the race, and cultural beliefs
3. swilling (72): drinking or eating greedily

**Scenes Five–Six, pp. 74–96**
1. vice squad (75): police squad responsible for enforcing laws against gambling and other forms of corruption
2. daemonic (75): demonic; of or caused by evil spirits
3. astrological (76): having to do with the study of the stars and planets to reveal their supposed influence on persons and/or events
4. contemptuously (77): scornfully; disdainfully
5. gossamer (84): a very thin, light cloth
6. coquettishly (84): flirtingly
7. neurasthenic (85): suffering from a neurosis accompanied by various aches and pains and characterized by extreme mental and physical fatigue; often accompanied by depression
8. stolid (85): not easily excited; impassive
9. Bohemian (88): one who lives an unconventional, carefree existence
10. alpaca (89): long, soft, silky wool from a llama
11. effeminate (95): lacking in manly qualities; womanish

### Scenes Seven–Eight, pp. 97–112
1. saccharine (98): sugary sweet
2. contrapuntally (98): interwoven with other sounds; e.g., a melody
3. contemptible (99): disgraceful; despicable
4. degenerate (102): a lower type; one who loses the normal and more highly developed moral characteristics

### Scenes Nine–Ten, pp. 113–130
1. uncavalier (113): not gallant or courteous to a lady
2. recriminations (119): counter accusations
3. spectral (122): ghostly
4. transitory (126): passing quickly; momentary
5. *sinously (128): moving or curving in a winding pattern; gracefully

*spelling in text*

### Scene Eleven, pp. 131–142
1. prodigiously (131): vastly; abnormally
2. quinine (136): a bitter drug used to treat malaria and fevers; muscle relaxant
3. aura (136): a subtle impression suggesting a specific surrounding or atmosphere
4. affectedly (137): put on for effect; artificially; exaggeratedly
5. colloquy (137): conversation; conference
6. sotto voce (139): in a low tone
7. voluptuously (142): sensually pleasurable

# Notes

# Notes